Acknowledgements

We owe a great deal to and have learned much from the teachers, schools, local authorities and national teams that we have worked with over the last decade. Our work with them has shaped our interpretation and ideas about formative assessment. Particular thanks go to the primary teachers on our Stockton Project and the Garth Olwg cluster whose examples we have used in the text.

1. What does this booklet offer?

Assessment lies at the heart of good teaching and learning. This is recognised in the Primary Framework (DCSF, 2008c):

Day-to-day assessment is a natural, integral and essential part of effective learning and teaching. Teachers and children continually reflect on how learning is progressing, see where improvements can be made and identify the next steps to take.

There is no shortage of encouragement – and pressure – for teachers to improve their work, raise their standards, improve children's attainment in test scores, and so on. Often, this advice has not taken into consideration the complexities involved

...pporting... their work. In reality, t... ...challenges that teachers face when a...mpting to offer guidance to thirty or more children in a classroom; advice which presents the situation in a simplistic way can be very disheartening for teachers.

This booklet focuses on how to develop assessment practice that helps improve learning within a primary school setting. We recognise that there are variations in policy and practice regarding assessment in Scotland, England, Wales and Northern Ireland, but maintain that the key components of good formative practice are relevant to all settings.

The recommendations that we make are illustrations of the principles that have been identified as key components of effective formative practice. They are grounded in both research findings and in our experience of working with many teachers, schools and local authorities over the last decade. We offer guidance on how to develop a community of learning, which builds on collaborative practice between children so that they can take the risks that are associated with new learning. This booklet includes examples of successful practice, over a range of subjects and ages, which practising teachers have found useful. These examples can be adapted to suit different age ranges, curriculum subjects or school

contexts because they utilise the basic principles of formative assessment.

Throughout the booklet, the terms 'children' and 'learners' are used to refer to all pupils, from those in early years setting of about three years of age through to pupils of 11 years of age who are at the end of their primary education. We also recognise that schools are establishments where qualified teachers work with a range of other adults – including classroom assistants and parents – the term 'teacher', therefore, refers to all those engaged with learners in the planned learning experiences.

In terms of coverage, Section 2 of this booklet presents the background history of the research and professional development work that the King's College team and others have been engaged in since the publication of *Inside the Black Box* (Black & Wiliam, 1998b). Sections 3 and 4 contextualise the work that follows by briefly outlining the primary setting and explaining the principles of learning that can be transformed into reality through formative practice.

Sections 5 to 7 set out in detail our findings on the main ways of practising formative assessment which we have found to be both workable and productive with primary teachers. These are complemented, in section 8, by discussion

of the particular problems of summative assessment and of opportunities for using the tools of summative assessment in a more formative fashion.

To close, section 9 discusses formulating a plan to support professional growth and learning towards a whole school approach to formative practice.

2. Background history

The findings on which this booklet is based have their origin in a review of research, published in 1998 both as a full article and in summary form as a short booklet for teachers (Black & Wiliam, 1998 a, b). This work established that there was strong evidence that formative assessment can raise standards of pupil achievement, but that the assessment practices entailed were not implemented in most classrooms. This led the group at King's College to explore the potential for practical improvement by collaborating with a group of teachers willing to take on the risks and extra work involved, with support from their schools and their LEAs. Through collaboration with the Medway and Oxfordshire LEAs, they were able to recruit six secondary schools spanning a range of catchment backgrounds. At the outset, twelve science and twelve mathematics teachers were involved; twelve teachers of English joined in the work at a later stage.

The first outcomes, which took almost two years to achieve, were that almost all of the teachers were positive about its effects for them, and that there were significant gains in test performance for the classes involved. On the basis of observations and records of visits to classrooms by the team, records of meetings of the whole group of teachers, interviews with and writing by the teachers themselves, and a few discussions with pupil groups, the group were able to summarise the findings in a second short booklet for teachers (Black et al. 2002). In addition, the group reported them at length both in a book (Black et al. 2003) and in many papers in professional and research journals.

Following the project, members of the King's team have made numerous contributions to teachers' conferences and to work with teachers and schools, both in professional development sessions, and in sustained follow-up work with individual schools. They have also been helping in developments on a larger scale, notably with the Scottish Educational Department, the States of Jersey and, more recently, with some Local Authorities in England, Scotland and Wales. Some of these professional development programmes have been in

a primary setting, others in secondary or cross-phase contexts. The development of formative assessment has influenced key initiatives for Key Stage 3 and the primary strategy materials and is acknowledged in the newly piloted QCA continuous summative initiative, Assessment for Pupil Progress (APP).

Throughout this work, we have always been aware that formative assessment has both *generic* features, i.e. features which apply to learning across all stages and all school subjects, and features which are *specific* – to primary teachers and to individual subjects. In this booklet, we hope to provide guidance and ideas for primary teachers based on extensive work with primary practitioners in professional development sessions and in schools.

We hope to provide insight not only of what teachers might try, but also to help teachers to evaluate their current practices and consider how to adapt and tackle aspects of this work. Over the last decade, the teachers we have worked with have invented and adapted a range of strategies to create a formative environment in their classrooms. While knowledge of these strategies is a good starting point for teachers wishing to develop their formative practice, it is important that sufficient time is given to introduce these into the classroom routines. On one point we are clear, and that is that each teacher needs to focus on the learning behaviours of their pupils and from this decide which strategies might help them become better learners. What each teacher makes of the ideas should be fashioned in a personal way to fit in with their individual approach to formative practice.

3. The aims of primary teaching

The education children receive during their primary schooling is crucial for both their personal development and for enculturing them into society. For the primary phase, the 'basics' of literacy and numeracy have always been regarded as pre-eminent, and this continues to hold not just in the UK but also internationally (University of Cambridge, 2008). In a government bid to raise standards, primary schools in England and Wales have undergone two decades of educational reform with a strong focus on numeracy and literacy. While this focus has changed how schools work, still much remains of the child-centred approach advocated by Plowden in the 1960s. The aims, values and purposes of primary education today combine the need to identify children's strengths and weaknesses, so as to provide help for them to develop as confident and resourceful learners, who both enjoy learning and also succeed in it. Child-centredness is thus seen as ensuring the growth of each individual child to contribute to, and work happily within, adult society.

In England, there are four themes that encapsulate the main principles primary schools are expected to nurture and address. These themes can be applied to all learners: that every child is unique; that caring loving support from parents and key adults provides the basis for a child to grow into a strong and independent learner; that the learning environment, both indoors and outdoors should be used to extend and challenge learning; and finally, a recognition that children learn in different ways and at different rates.

It is well documented that successful Early Years education uses structured and unstructured play sessions where the individual can develop social skills and explore their natural curiosity with carefully mediated adult intervention (EPPE 2004: *A Statutory Framework for the Early Years Foundation Stage 2007*, DCSF 2008b). This process is honed and refined over an extended time period until children reach a stage where they benefit from a higher proportion of structured activities with a greater emphasis on acquiring a set of effective learning behaviours. When coupled with higher order questions that challenge children's perception of the world around them, this helps them reconstruct understanding.

All this is set within a context that intrigues and an environment that supports their particular stage of development and interests (see *Excellence & Enjoyment: A strategy for primary schools*, DfES 2003; *A Curriculum for Excellence*, SEED 2004; *A Framework for Children's Learning for 3 to 7-year-olds in Wales*, DCELLS 2008). This process is further developed in infant and junior classroom settings, where teachers are able to build on these early experiences and refine and develop the children's collaborative learning behaviours, helping them to take a proactive role in their learning journey.

From the earliest ages to the end of primary education, effective learning is about using a broad curriculum as a vehicle to deepen understanding rather than providing rote learning that leads the children towards memorising correct answers. This involves identifying where children are in their learning and deciding on the best learning experiences through which the children can take their next steps. It also requires the teacher to utilise the curiosity and enthusiasm with which children come to school and to foster this so that children are encouraged to take on an active learning role. Using a formative approach enables skilled teachers to check on learning and to develop experiences that address areas of misunderstanding or gaps in knowledge, while enhancing proficiency in a range of skills for lifelong independent learning. Formative assessment fits well into this learning scenario, since its purpose is for teachers to both generate and sift the rich data that arises in class discussion and activity, so that professional judgements can be made about the next steps in learning. Feedback, peer and self-assessment all have important roles to play in this process and utilised properly, formative assessment can enhance learning.

4. Principles of learning

Assessment **FOR** learning is about improvement and should not be confused with assessment for accountability or monitoring processes, often called 'assessment **OF** learning'. The Assessment Reform Group's 1999 publication, *Beyond the Black Box*, summarised assessment for learning as:

- *Embedded in the teaching and learning experience*
- *Sharing learning goals with the learners*
- *Helping pupils to know and to recognise the standards they are aiming for*
- *Pupils being engaged in self-assessment*
- *Providing feedback which leads the learner to recognise the next steps and how to take them*
- *Underpinned by the belief that every learner can improve*

- *Involving both the teacher and learner reviewing and reflecting on the assessment information*

The **first** principle of learning is to start from where the learner is. This also recognises that children have to be active in the learning process and need to construct their ideas from the many experiences they have gained both in and out of school. It is also clear that to merely add to those ideas an overlay of new ideas leads to poor understanding and confusion. These may not surface until much later in their education and by then ideas are strongly held and much harder to relinquish.

Discussion is not enough: the teacher has to encourage and to listen carefully to a range of responses, taking them all seriously whether they are right or wrong, and then help children to talk through inconsistencies and to respond to challenges. In such discussion, the teachers are tailoring their interventions to meet the learning needs that have been made evident, but they are also implementing a **second** principle of learning, which is that students must be active in the process – learning has to be done *by* them, it cannot be done *for* them. The children have to close the gap between what they don't know and what they want to know and they need to be taught the skills to 'close the gap'.

A **third** principle is that in order to learn, children must understand the purpose of the learning both in the short term and the long term, which requires detailed understanding of what counts as 'good quality work'. They must also have an idea of where they stand in relation to this ultimate goal. Only with these two ideas can they work towards meta-cognition, which is the power to oversee and steer their own learning in the right direction, so that they can take responsibility for it. This is often termed as 'thinking about their thinking' and is no small achievement. It requires attention in teaching to help children understand the focus of their learning and to understand the criteria for quality, i.e. to be able to tell where their efforts do or do not meet the agreed criteria. Peer- and self-assessment are essential here, for they promote both active involvement and practice in making judgments about the quality of work – both their own and that of their peers.

For young and inexperienced learners this process can be carefully developed over an extended period of time using a series of steps, each small enough for the target to be meaningful to the pupil, yet big enough to be a challenging step along the route of progression. Self confidence is developed alongside the skills necessary to recognise the next steps for improvement. Even very young children have been found to be capable of thinking about how they feel about their learning and, over a longer period of time, they become more able to reflect on the learning in relation to the agreed criteria.

Fourthly, when children are talking about their learning, whether in pairs, small groups or whole-classes, they are able to use specific and precise vocabulary. 'Talking the talk' is an important part of learning that can be supported by teacher mediation and builds on the words used by a child and their peers. Children learn through talk, and as children talk, they also provide valuable evidence to enable the teacher to diagnose where they are in their learning. Ascertaining what children partly know and understand is the key to planning future steps in their learning. So planning, on a simple level, requires the teacher to find activities that encourage children to talk. This includes knowledge of the potential of learning tasks for exploring children's understanding and a willingness to monitor and regulate learning as it is taking place.

This work is largely centred on the idea that children learn through collaborative exploration (Vygotsky, 1978), sometimes learning from more knowledgeable peers while, at other times, helping their peers to understand. In order to tune into the areas where some uncertainties lie, it is important that the activities in which the children engage are quite challenging for those learners. In some cases, this involves the children applying current understanding within a new context or from a different viewpoint. In others, it encourages deeper understanding as the children have to make connections using their existing knowledge.

It is also important to think about how feedback affects the motivation and self-esteem of children. Feedback can be of two kinds. In the **first kind**, it focuses on the child as a good or bad achiever, emphasising overall judgment by marks, grades, rank-order lists, and so on. This helps to develop what researchers have called ego-involvement, and its effects are negative. It discourages the low-attainers, but it also makes high-attainers avoid tasks if they cannot easily see their way to success, for failure would be seen as bad news about themselves rather than as an opportunity to learn. In the **second kind**, the focus is not on the person but on the strengths and weaknesses of the particular piece of work, emphasising what needs to be done to improve. This helps to develop task-involvement practices. Its effects are positive for it can encourage all children, whatever their past achievements, that they can do better by trying, and that they can learn from mistakes and failures (for the evidence, see Dweck, 2000).

5. Implementing formative assessment

In this section we will look at the various aspects of classroom practice that need to be worked on to enable formative assessment to be developed effectively. First, we will briefly look at the **role of dialogue** in the classroom. This will lead us on to look at **rich questions and activities** as a means of evoking good evidence while stimulating pupils' involvement in their learning. What is important here is that children reveal their thinking through talk and this can be stimulated by pictures, artefacts and objects or by a rich question or scenario to which the children are asked to respond. The third part looks at **encouraging children to respond** and the various approaches to improving peer discussion. Finally, the crux of the work is the way that the teacher handles the various contributions from the learners by **responding to or using pupils' contributions**. This is what constitutes a formative approach to talk – a rich question or activity on its own is not formative, and the real challenge is to judge what to do with what arises in the classroom talk. It is therefore essential that teachers think about how to deal with the children's responses and contributions to the discussion. It is this response that will shape each learner's understanding and the way that learners value themselves and others within the learning environment.

The role of dialogue

Through talk, children can both reveal their current thoughts and, by responding to the ideas of others, begin to construct new ways of thinking about a topic or a skill. Robin Alexander in his booklet *Towards Dialogic Teaching* (2004) argues that:

Children, we now know, need to talk, and to experience a rich diet of spoken language, in order to think and to learn. Reading, writing and number may be the acknowledged curriculum 'basics' but talk is arguably the true foundation of learning. (p. 5)

Alexander also categorised the different types of talk that he witnessed in an international comparison of primary classrooms as:

- rote – drilling of facts, ideas and routines
- recitation – questions designed to elicit recall or work out answers from clues in the question
- instruction/exposition – giving information and explaining facts, principles and procedures

- discussion – exchange of ideas with a view to sharing information and solving problems
- dialogue – seeking common understanding through questioning and discussion which guide and prompt, reduce choices, minimise risk and error and expedite 'handover' of concepts and principles (p. 33).

While teachers need to use all of these types of talk for particular purposes in their lessons, it is clear that for encouraging thinking and developing a formative approach within the classroom, much of the talk should be centred around the two latter categories of discussion and dialogue. This requires the teacher to select activities where the children talk purposefully in groups. What is paramount in this process is the children realising that their thinking is valued by the teacher, so that they are encouraged to discuss their understanding and misunderstandings openly.

Opportunities for sustained periods of quality talk to tease out learners' own understandings and build on each other's ideas are needed across the whole age range, and for all; including those who do not have English as their first language. Younger learners, or those with short attention spans due to special educational needs, have been found to benefit from frequent short sessions of self review, with concrete examples to refer to. These groups of children also need greater opportunity to talk in mediated pairs compared to older or more experienced learners.

Rich questions and activities

Questions have a range of roles to play in the classroom, from organisational and managerial, to encouraging the construction of new understanding. A shift away from organisational and instructional questions towards questions that promote discussion and collaboration ensures that the formative opportunities in classrooms are maximised. Rich questions provide opportunity for thinking and discussion. In the national project that we supported in Scotland from 2002–2004, some children called such questions 'fat questions', since the answers required five words or more. The opposite of this is a 'skinny question', which generally requires only a few, or a single word to answer it.

Examples of fat questions

- *If Red Riding Hood's grandmother had been out, what might the wolf have done?*
- *If you keep a drink with ice cubes in a thermos flask, how much room do you need to leave for the ice cubes to melt?*
- *How many ways can I make 10?*
- *Which is the 'odd-one-out' – bird, cat, fish, and elephant? Why?*
- *Which is the 'odd-one out' – forward roll,*

handstand, jump, bunnyhop? Why?
- *A church is like a school because . . .?*
- *Which is the best material for Teddy's hat? How do you know?*
- *Which instrument would you choose for the magician's part? How would you play it?*

Through formative questioning, the teacher hopes that the children's talk will reveal rich evidence of the children's understanding, including what they know and also, their partly formed ideas. Teaching is about helping youngsters realise where they are and then guiding them to upgrade their part-knowledge to a fuller understanding. Formative assessment is about moving knowledge and understanding forward and providing a means for helping children do this.

Some teachers believe that they need to avoid 'closed' questions in the classroom. This is not always the case. Sometimes it is important to get the children to make a decision about an idea so that you can probe their understanding further. In a Year 1 science session, the teacher asked the children to decide if they thought that the shadow got *bigger* or *smaller* the nearer the object was to the light. Asking the children to place a tick on the board beneath the words smaller or bigger, or to put a card with their name on into the appropriately labelled boxes provided the starting point for a discussion about 'why'.

Doing an experiment or other activity and then coming back to see if ideas have changed builds on this further and allows youngsters to see when their ideas are changing.

Teachers are able to mediate and extend the talk by thought-provoking questions. For example, the speech bubbles in the figure below, show children's reactions to a picture stimulus.

The questions below can be used to probe children's ideas further and to encourage the them to talk.

Questions of clarification:

- *What do you mean by that?*
- *Say a bit more.*
- *Can you give us an example?*

Questions that probe assumptions:

- *Why would someone say that?*
- *What do you think happened?*

Questions that probe reason and evidence:

- *What are your reasons for saying that?*
- *Are you saying . . .?*
- *Which means . . .?*

Questions that probe implications and consequences:

- *What might happen if you did this . . . not that . . .?*
- *What other reasons might there be for that happening?*

Questions about viewpoints or perspectives:

- *What would be another way of saying that?*
- *How do Sian's ideas differ from Gashan's?*

Questions about the question:

- *What other questions might be useful?*
- *Can you explain how that question is going to help us?*

Another set of strategies that have been used to support talk are 'learning walls' and 'question trees'. Here, questions that interest individuals about a chosen topic are collected from the children and stuck on either the 'learning wall' or 'question tree'. This technique can be used even with young children as they can draw their question on a 'sticky note' and explain the question to the class as it is stuck on

the wall/tree. As learning takes place, the children are asked to select from the 'learning wall' or 'question tree' questions they now feel they can answer.

Encouraging children to respond

Demanding questions require time for the learner to think about what they are being asked, to think what the question means and then to formulate a suitable reply. For some questions, this can be achieved by increasing the wait time (the time between a teacher asking a question and taking an answer). Rowe (1974) found that the wait time in primary science classes was very low, less than one second. Studies in secondary schools have shown that increasing the wait time by 3–5 seconds produced a dramatic effect on the involvement of the students in classroom discussion. Rowe's research showed that increased wait time led to:

- longer answers being given than previously
- more pupils electing to answer
- fewer pupils refusing to answer
- pupils commenting on or adding to the answers of other children
- more alternative explanations or examples being offered.

Creating the classroom culture where children of all ages feel they can reveal current understanding and be helped to firmer understanding is an essential ingredient to making formative assessment function in the classroom. Peer discussion plays an essential part in creating such a supportive, formative environment. The opportunity to discuss ideas within a small group helps learners articulate and check ideas before they reveal their group's answer to the whole class. Answers are better formed through the group activity and also, if an answer is incorrect or limited, then it feels less threatening to the individual as it is their group's decision and not theirs alone. Skills need to be developed and practised to achieve this.

Children are often reluctant to commit to an answer because they are shy about speaking out in class, or are reluctant to reveal their inadequacies to the teacher and to their peers. The teacher's role when formative questions are asked is to act as a facilitator – encouraging children to try to answer and also to listen carefully to the answers from their peers. It is important to create a classroom environment in which children are willing to share their emerging ideas. While talk has a role in enhancing and ensuring cognitive development, it also has a role helping children regulate their learning. Learners know when they do not understand the ideas arising within a learning situation.

We found that in some classrooms, even when wait time was increased, some pupils were reluctant to offer answers and in other classrooms, there were pupils who found it hard not to dominate the talk which inhibited others from speaking. To try and engage more learners in answering, a number of techniques were developed. Some teachers managed the process by asking the children to jot down an answer either on a piece of paper or a mini whiteboard, so that when asked by the teacher to answer they either would read out or hold up their answer. Other teachers adopted a 'no hands up' strategy, taking the view that if sufficient wait time was given, then everyone should be expected to answer when they selected individuals. Other teachers used red and green cards so that learners could indicate with the green card either that they knew the answer, or by showing both, that they might know, and indicating with the red card that they did not know. In this strategy, learners often changed their choice of card as they listened to the answers of their peers because either their own ideas were challenged or consolidated or, in some cases, a vital part of a peer's answer enabled them to complete their own thinking.

A number of strategies have been developed by teachers to help learners take a more active role in classroom talk. Think-Pair-Share is a method where children turn to the child sitting next to them to discuss the question being asked. This allows for exchange of ideas, sharing of vocabulary and an opportunity to formulate an answer through collaborative peer talk before sharing with the whole class. Some teachers refer to this strategy as 'using talk buddies' or 'sharing with talking partners' within a learning discussion.

Some children remain reluctant to answer in class, even if they use Think-Pair-Share to talk in groups. One way of overcoming this shyness or resentment at being selected to speak has been using lollipop sticks with the children's names on. These are picked out of a pot and the fact that children see this as being randomly selected, somehow convinces them to have a go at the answer. This method can also limit the child who tends to dominate the classroom talk, as it is seen as a fair way of being selected. An alternative, but similar system that some teachers used was to take two packs of playing cards and to take out the aces, royals and some number cards to leave the same number of cards as children in the class. The teacher would distribute one pack to individuals in the class and keep one set for herself. She could then select a card from her pack and the child with the matching card would answer. An ICT version of this is to use a name loop that contains all the children's names, each on a page. These pages are then rotated at speed and can be stopped to reveal the name of the child selected to answer.

With young children, it takes considerable time and effort to encourage them to talk about a chosen topic in groups and in whole class situations, as they are still at an egocentric stage. The challenge with very young children is that they are often shy and also lack the vocabulary to discuss at length. They need to develop the skills in developing the type of talk that is required here and also the willingness to engage in discussion, particularly active listening. One Year 2 teacher helped develop this in her class by creating 'when, where, who, and why' cards for her pupils. A selection of these cards were given out to the children and when the teacher worked with the whole class, she would stop talking at various points and say:

'Who can ask a "what" question here?'
Or
'Perhaps we need a "why" question here?'

Those children with the appropriate 'what' or 'why' cards would try and formulate a question using the starting word they had been given. The other children would both judge which of the questions were good questions and also contribute the answer. In this way, the teacher was introducing the skills of questioning and listening needed for peer discussion.

Other teachers have worked on developing children's discussion skills through helping children to ask questions in class. Changing 'show and tell' activities into 'show and ask' activities, or incorporating puppets into the classroom talk can encourage children to ask more questions and to listen carefully to what others have to say. Some teachers have incorporated games to help this development. One game to encourage peer discussion is to allow one child to see a hidden object and then the others ask that child questions to find out what the object is like. Teachers can support the skill development here by helping the children focus so that they might recognise good questions or spot those occasions where a child had listened and built on a previous question or answer.

With older children, it is a brave learner who attempts to think aloud and make public the fact that they cannot engage with the shared meaning that is evolving in the dialogue. Rather, learners withdraw from the dialogue or listen in, hoping to re-engage with the sense-making. If, however, such learners can find the confidence to offer their pre-understanding or emergent understanding, then the group engaged in the dialogue can react to this and so allow the learner to examine and then re-examine the sense they are making of the shared meaning. It is only through entering the dialogue about shared ideas that the learner can begin to see other aspects of the ideas and so make judgements about where they are in their own sense-making. Non-engagement not only deprives the group of the learner's position but also prevents the learner from revealing their own sense-making to themselves. However, if a learner does offer their emergent understanding, then they are at the mercy of their dialogic partners since movement forwards rests on the reaction from others. If agreement with or challenge to the learner's emergent ideas is not forthcoming from the group, then there is no selection pressure to help the learner reflect on and shape their understanding. This leaves the learner in a vulnerable position where they have revealed both publicly and to themselves where their thinking is but without a means of moving forward through the guidance and challenge from the others engaged in the dialogue; it therefore becomes difficult for the learner to continue to engage with both the problem and with the dialogue. Active participation in dialogue can therefore be a risky business for individual learners.

Responding to or using pupils' contributions

Creating a climate where probing questions and discussion are integral to the learning process is not an easy role to play for some teachers. Children readily look to the teacher to articulate and check and so pass judgement on answers either by their comments, body language or facial expressions. While it is important to sort out misconceptions and incorrect ideas, teachers have found that waiting for the various ideas and thoughts to be revealed before they start correcting and curbing the direction of the discussion, allows for greater child interaction and thoughtful reflection. If intervention comes too soon, then not only do many of the misplaced ideas fail to be revealed but there may be too little opportunity for the learner to reflect on what is being discussed alongside what they think. This process of 'thinking about their thinking' is called meta-cognition and takes time to develop.

Sometimes, teachers need to work on strategies to prevent them 'cutting off' classroom talk. This mostly involves teachers temporarily withholding their judgement about an answer from the children so that the learners can compare answers given by other children with the answers they hold inside their heads. For example, one of the maths questions that a couple of different Year 6 classes discussed was:

'What's similar and what's different about fractions and ratios?'

The first teacher used a technique called 'Pose-Pause-Pounce-Bounce'. First, the teacher poses the question. Then there is a pause for thinking (wait time) before she selects a child to answer. On hearing the first answer, the teacher immediately bounces the question to a second child. The 'pounce-bounce' action prevents the teacher reacting to the first answer and so possibly cutting off the class talk. The second child might give the same or a different answer to the first and may or may not respond to what was said in the first answer. Whatever happens, the point is that the classroom talk has started to move away from the teacher judging publicly whether the answer is correct to the voicing of more student talk and ideas. The ultimate aim of many of these teachers is to achieve several 'bounces' before they intervene. This pushes the talk in the direction of the learners, which in itself is beneficial to learning, but also gives the teacher information about the current state of learning. This technique also provides essential 'thinking time', during which the teacher can plan what intervention is needed to help drive the learning forward.

A second teacher approached the collection of her Year 6 class ideas differently. She posed the same question:

'What's similar and what's different about fractions and ratios?'

She then asked her class to discuss the question in groups so that they would be able to explain these similarities and differences in terms of sharing a large pizza. After five minutes of group talk, during which the teacher circulated and listened in on snippets of the dialogue, she asked each group in turn to articulate one main point or idea that had arisen within their group talk. Two children acted as scribes writing up these thoughts on the board. The teacher repeated what each group said to help the scribes and to help others in the class hear the point. She then asked the groups to talk about the various points that had been written on the board – which did they agree with, which needed more clarity to make sense, which did they disagree with? The teacher circulated the groups, listening into the conversation without intervention, verbally or non-verbally.

The teacher then orchestrated a whole class discussion by asking a specific group to begin to explain what decisions a family have to come to in cutting up the large pizza. In the whole-class discussion, the teacher was able to select groups that had had interesting ideas or uncertainties during the group discussion and so these ideas were aired for a second time with a wider audience. This meant that children were able to challenge or consolidate their developing ideas. From these interactions, the teacher was able to gauge individual, group and class understanding while the learners had their ideas continually reviewed and challenged. This reciprocity in learning was only possible through the medium of talk; written communication separates the assessment from the learning in time and reduces the possibilities for shared purpose.

6. Feedback for 'feedforward'

For assessment to be formative the feedback information has to be used.

(Black & Wiliams, 1998)

In classrooms where talk is emphasised, children are receiving continual feedback about their developing ideas and learning. There are also times when teachers wish to feedback on particular pieces of work that the children produce. This feedback will provide guidance for improvement.

In many cases, the feedback comment relates back to the description of quality that has been discussed by the children before they attempt a task. In this way, children work towards success or quality by considering the criteria as their work progresses. The feedback is then the teacher's judgement matched against the child's own judgement of quality. Mostly, comments encourage children to reflect on what they have produced and provide guidance for improvement. For example, if a child is asked to describe and explain, then effective comments might be:

- *Your use of adjectives to describe the old lady is good. Now use the same approach to describe the house saying how it looks and sounds.*
- *Think about the reasons why the box was unstable and give some advice for the next class who are going to make these.*
- *Tell me why you selected a blue background and how a red or a brown background might change the mood.*
- *Good use of pictures in your brochure. Which do **you** think is the most important one to support your idea?*

Useful prompts to encourage specific improvements might be:

- *Tell us more about . . .*
- *Use another sentence/word/digit/picture here so that . . .*
- *Use one of these words . . . or one of your own to describe . . .*
- *Explain a bit more about . . .*
- *Describe how . . .*
- *How else can you . . .*

Sometimes, comments can be used to direct children where to go for help:

- *Look back at the way we worked out . . . and pinpoint the mistake you are making.*
- *Go back to our work on 30th January and check how you used the decimal point there. Compare it with what you have done here.*
- *You are mixing up 'there' and 'their'. First check your glossary for an explanation. Then rewrite the first three sentences to show that you have got it.*
- *Some good adverbs used here. Take a look at how Amy has used them with other 'juicy' words. Ask her to help you improve this last paragraph.*

Sometimes, comments are used to consolidate developing ideas and skills:

- *This is a much better opening sentence. Well done. Now think about a good way to end it, too.*
- *More keywords used in your explanations. It might help you remember to use them if you highlight them. Which colour do you think would be best for this?*
- *Your maps are much clearer. Think what you have done to achieve this and make a note in your Learning Log.*

Comments for younger children are usually given orally or read to them by the teacher. However, one Reception teacher successfully created a guidance code with her class, which meant that they could read it for themselves. This not only gave a written record for them to look back at and reflect on, but it also provided a narrative for tracking progress.

She devised the following codes with the children over the year:

- A small square box represented 'leave a space'.

- A pink crayon mark indicated where the learning target had been hit (the teacher would say this meant she was 'tickled pink' by their achievement).

- 'AW' was a reminder to use their action words which were taken from the key 45 words children should know.

'AW'

- A small box with 'S' inside meant they needed to use their 'spell it book' which is their own book where their words are attempted and correct spelling given.

S

- A zigzag line indicated 'write more'.

- A little stick man running meant 'work faster'.

- A capital 'B' crossed out and 'b' ticked meant they need to use lower case.

B   b√

The opportunity to react to and act on comments is essential, particularly when a formative way of working is being introduced to a class. The learners need to recognise that the teacher really does want a piece of work improved and wants to ensure that progress is being made. This means providing opportunity within lesson time for learners to read or hear comments on their work and to identify with their peers and teacher the specific improvements which are needed. It is useful to allocate time, for the improvements to be made, in class at regular intervals. This is especially true for young learners who will find it hard to remember from one lesson to the next. Encouraging children to see their work as 'under construction' rather than reaching a final product will help them to make appropriate gains over a period of time. The teacher may also wish to note, in their own ongoing assessment records for a child, the feedback given, which will help to build up a picture of that child's overall view of attainment at key points in the year.

One simple way that was devised to support the development of improving work through comment-only marking was to attach the top of an A4 sheet of paper into the back cover of the pupil's book. The sheet then contains an accumulation of comments and allows both the pupil and teacher to recognise where improvements have been made or where specific problems are arising. In some cases, this comment sheet became a written dialogue between the teacher and the learner. Another method was to use 'sticky notes' which can be stuck at the relevant places. These can be removed by the teacher or child once the comments have been addressed. Another variation was for the teacher to highlight children's work for either strengths, weaknesses or a mixture of these. The child was then able to gauge the quality of their work and recognise where they needed to work to improve.

Encouraging a dialogue between teacher and child can be enhanced when the child feels able to identify his own areas for help. Simple strategies can be used: 'traffic lighting' their own work to indicate how confident they feel having completed the task, or writing specific comments to the teacher. Such recognition by children initiates the desire to sort out their uncertainty and encourage feedback and so learning is moved forward. Feedback drives formative action. The examples below show the sort of pupil comments that we have seen:

- *I can see how to chunk in questions 1, 2 and 3 but not too sure in the others.*
- *I have done my acrostic poem, but can't remember if it needs to have rhymes as well.*
- *Can you start with a connective?*
- *Thanks. I get it now!*

The ultimate user of assessment information is the learner and the culture needed in the classroom to support and encourage the learner is one of success, backed by a belief that all can achieve. Whilst assessment can help all learners, it gives particularly good results with low-attainers, where it concentrates on specific problems with their work. Comments give the learner a clear understanding of what is wrong along with appropriate guidance for the next steps for improvement. These steps and a means of achieving them in the short term are what moves the learning forward. It is essential that the message within the feedback comment focuses on achievement and improvement of specific pieces of work to avoid such learners losing sight of their long-term goal or being inhibited from attempting to reach it because of overtones of comparison and competition. One method of finding the correct balance and tone to encourage redrafting small sections of work and helping further improvement is the 'Two Stars and a Wish' or the 'Box and Bubble' approach (shown overleaf), where strengths are clearly identified followed by specific next step guidance:

- *You remembered your finger spaces and capital letters. Now try to put in your full stops too.*
- *Circuit diagrams are clear and you recognise parallel and series circuits. Can you also explain why the bulbs are brighter in the parallel circuit?*
- *Detailed drawings and clear descriptions. Now add a few words to explain how these are used in the various ceremonies.*

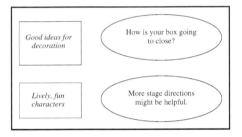

'Box and Bubble'

While there is a great deal of evidence to suggest that developing formative practices will improve learning, putting such practices into reality, in the classroom, requires teachers to have a particular mindset and a repertoire of skills at their fingertips. These include a willingness to monitor learning as it is taking place, rather than simply measure it at the end of the learning period. Linked to this, is a need for effective feedback mechanisms that foster self-reflection in children and encourage them to work at improvement. Receiving feedback will only lead to improvement if the child is provided with an opportunity to try out an idea for a second time or, indeed, several times. Each time a child tries out a similar activity, she can hone her approach and gradually progress towards competency. In other words, she is gradually 'closing the gap' and moving towards the next stage in her understanding.

When teachers share with children suggestions for the next steps in learning and how they might take them, children are more likely to understand what they need to do to improve. However, unless opportunities are provided for them to take those next steps in their learning soon after they have received feedback, they may not remember what they need to do and may not develop the skills and strategies for taking those next learning steps. A cycle of iteration is required in which next learning steps are identified and communicated, followed by interpretation and negotiation of these next steps and then further renegotiation as pupils undertake these steps in a subsequent activity. For the teacher, this means organising the curriculum in a way that sets up an iterative process in which feedback and informed attempts can help the pupil make progress. Such an approach may be at odds with a curriculum that is planned for coverage.

Formative feedback is about moving learning forward. This can be done orally or in writing. Marks, National Curriculum levels, grades or reward systems on work have no place in a formative environment because:

- learners do not get the specific advice on how the learning can be improved
- they emphasise competition between learners not personal improvement: this discourages their collaborative learning, reduces the likelihood of their taking risks and can limit sharing what they definitely know rather than their tentative current thinking
- they demotivate low attainers and give no challenge to high attainers who are reluctant to take a risk in case they are incorrect.

Some teachers may be inclined to compromise by using National Curriculum levels together with comments. However, research (Butler, 1987) indicates that this is a waste of time on the teacher's part because the children focus on the mark or level and fail to read the guidance comment. We have also noticed that teachers' comments become more detailed and targeted once they stop using grades or levels. This may be because they have more time to spend on deciding on the comment rather than assigning a grade or level, or that they realise that the comments are the main communication to the child and must be informative. Effective feedback should help the learner know where they are in their learning journey and where they should go next for improvement.

While there was initially resistance by some teachers to the increase in time needed for the writing of effective feedback, this quickly changed as they could see how the children came to realise that these type of activities provided the starting point for the teacher coaching them towards better understanding. Teachers realised that the reason why it is easier to comment on some activities than others was generally because some activities were more challenging than others and often required reasoning rather than simple recall. Many teachers decided that they would concentrate their feedback on these more challenging activities and the simple recall tasks were just checked in class by the children. This enabled teachers to give fewer comments, but more effective ones.

7. Self- and peer-assessment

Planning for formative assessment needs to be considered as part of the work in making the children more actively responsible for their learning. To help them do this, they need to know what learning is expected of them and how this builds on what they have learnt already. There are a variety of ways that teachers can do this. Shirley Clarke's early work (2001) encouraged teachers to use two characters, WALT (We Are Learning Today) and WILF (What I am Looking For . . .) which not only focused the children on the learning but also provided a framework for feedback and reflection later in the lesson.

An example of WALT and WILF is:

We Are Learning Today in history about Victorian children's lives.

What I am Looking For are children who can explain the difference between the toys Victorian children played with and the ones we play with today.

Other teachers have used KWL grids where pupils decide what they already 'Know', what they 'Want to know' and to which they can return later to recognise 'what they have Learnt.' Yet other practitioners create activities using Keyword Cards – cards on which keywords for a topic are written. Small groups of children first decide which of the keywords they know and which they don't. The latter cards are returned to the teacher to help plan for future learning.

For the Keyword Cards they know, the children are asked to take it in turns to tell one another one thing about the keyword and they continue doing this until they can find no more to say. The teacher can listen into these conversations and tune in to where the strengths and weaknesses lie for particular children or groups of children within a specific topic, and then use this information to inform future planning. At the same time, the learners are tuning in to where they need to concentrate their efforts to improve, as they become more aware of their learning and their own needs.

The information from both the KWL grids and the Keyword Cards can be used for short-term and medium-term planning by the teacher and these plans can be altered and updated as the children progress through the topic. In other words, plans tend to get messy as time goes on, because it is impossible to predict exactly how much time individuals, groups and classes require to sort out their learning. Experienced teachers will have an idea of concepts or skills that children of that age often struggle with and can plan ahead 'gaps' in anticipation. Formative planning creates opportunity for review and so the pace of work is driven by the progress in learning.

Some teachers have more radically changed the way they plan to encourage the children to take a more active part in the formative process. The Year 1 and Year 4 teachers in one school changed their planning approach from the October half term onwards. Having spent two months getting to know their children and helping their children work more collaboratively, they began a planning approach which required them to plan activities for Monday up to Thursday lunchtime. Thursday afternoon was used as a reflection on the week's work, where children, helped by their teachers, looked through the work they had done and discussed how confident they were in what they had achieved. The children decided what things they felt they had done well and on which areas they needed to do some more work. The teachers then provided support and extension activities for the next day and the children worked in a more individual way for the Friday. The agreement was that the children could have Golden Time (where they selected their own activities) once the support or extension work had been completed to both the teacher and pupil's satisfaction. There were several occasions when children elected to do more sums or to have another go at a piece of writing, when the teacher would have allowed them their Golden Time. This type of behaviour is indicative of children who are 'switched on to learning'.

Another way into planning formatively is to use Learning Intentions with the children. Some teachers call these Learning Objectives: these are statements which outline the expectations for the learning in an activity or a lesson or, sometimes, a series of lessons. In English, the Learning Intention might be: 'to use connectives effectively in our story.' In science, it might be: 'to work out which position was best for our seedlings to grow.' In art, it might be: 'to sketch in the style of Lowry.' From the Learning Intention, the children are able to work out what they need to achieve as an outcome and these are called the success criteria. For the above Learning Intentions, the success criteria might be 'to have more than three different connectives that help the flow of my story', 'to use a table or bar chart to explain which position was best' and 'to produce a sketch that shows the dark mood and simple shapes, like those of Lowry.'

Both the Learning Intentions and the success criteria need to be discussed and shared with the children so that they can internalise what it all means in terms of quality and expectations. The timing of this process will depend on the dynamics of the activity. When to do this will depend on what previous knowledge and understanding the class have of that aspect of learning. In the

English example above, the children need to have some experience of writing that is stilted by lack of connectives as well as some that flows because of the connectives, so that they can have an inkling of what the Learning Intention is asking of them. If they had previously had this within another activity, then they will be more likely to recognise this from the outset and can understand and use the success criteria from the start of the activity. However, if they have not had this previous experience leading up to this activity, then this needs to be planned into the learning experience and the success criteria formulated with the children part-way through the lesson. In the art example above, it would be pointless asking children what they thought the success criteria would be before they had seen, discussed and recognised the key features of a Lowry painting. But having done this, the children will be able to describe specific features that should be included or excluded from the sketch and this can be used to decide the criteria for success. In the science example, it might help for some children to think about and discuss how they could present findings in a clear and concise way based on prior knowledge before they decide on or see the success criteria, as these are meant to summarise expectations and instil a sense of what quality means. Success criteria should not be presented as a checklist provided by the teacher, because the children may respond to this in a mechanistic manner that does not affect their own sense of learning and of quality.

It needs to be noted here that Learning Outcomes, which are used in the Primary Strategy documentation, are not the same as Learning Intentions. Learning Outcomes list the products you expect from the children's work and not the learning. Learning outcomes tend to be 'tangible', i.e. 'At the end of this lesson you will each have a sketch.' In the science example it would be: 'You will each have a set of measurements' in English it might be: 'You will each have written at least four sentences.' This is used as a way of giving an overall understanding of expectations. Learning outcomes such as 'to write four sentences' are often used in primary classrooms to encourage pace as the teacher can chivvy slow workers by reminding the children that 'you should have two written by now'. Learning Outcomes could be of a larger scale, e.g. in history it could be: 'At the end of this topic you will each have a topic folder with writing and pictures about aspects of how the Victorians lived compared with today. Each topic folder will look different because you will include something you want to explore for yourself.'

Self-assessment has an essential role to play in formative practice. The skills associated with this have to be taught and take some time to become fully developed. Teachers have used a range of approaches to create the sort of climate that builds into effective learning behaviours. This has often included the orchestration of talk about the task linked to their emotional response such as: 'Tell your partner what made you think this was easy or difficult'. As children become more proficient in this self-reflective process, so the teacher will be able to shift the focus towards improvement rather than reflection. Young children, and those with English as an additional language, will require simplified questioning with supplementary questions such as: 'Was that hard or easy?' It is accepted that young children will find it tricky to consider work that is not their own, but even they are capable of recognising what they like and don't like and this is the start of developing a sense of quality.

Self-assessment and peer-assessment go hand in hand with each other and both require time to talk about the process and the product. Teachers can create wonderful lessons by facilitating debates on ideas and providing guidance on the next learning steps but it is only the learner who can do the learning; it cannot be done for them by the teacher. In other words, children need to learn how to self-assess.

This is not a simple task as it requires them to have a sufficiently clear picture, of the purpose as well as of the desired outcome, and also a means of moving forward to close the learning gap. In some classrooms, children do not have this clear picture and respond to lessons as a set of exercises to be completed. In this scenario, the learners are not fully engaged with the learning and are not aware of the rationale behind specific tasks. So finding their way through to attain their individual targets is a non-starter. However, when children do have such overview, they then become more committed and effective learners.

Through our work with teachers, we have found that peer-assessment helps learners develop and hone their self-assessment skills. Learners have the ability to recognise both quality and inadequacies in other peoples' work even if the level of competence at which they themselves are performing differs from the level of work which they are evaluating. With careful coaching using clear criteria for quality, children can begin to develop awareness of success and identify problem areas in specific pieces of work and to articulate these to each other. This is clearly enhanced if they are also regularly receiving effective guidance comments from their teacher as this provides the language, style and model to help them discuss their work with one another and so provide feedback. Ideas for improvement are not isolated statements but are assimilated into the child's growing idea about work quality, so that peer discussion about work enables each child to see the strengths and weaknesses of their own work with greater clarity. Such practice also encourages them to improve pieces of work as they begin to see how small changes, additions or different ways of approaching parts of the work can easily raise the overall quality of their work; it is the regular small pushes forward that help embed better learning behaviours and raise overall attainment.

As with other formative assessment techniques, pupils need training: starting in a small way and evolving their practice gradually is the best way forward. One way found to be successful was to start with simple checking of work and so once a week children swapped books and checked each others work against simple straightforward criteria such as:

- capital letter at the start of each sentence
- full stop at the end of each sentence
- date and title underlined
- new paragraph for each new idea
- capital letters for the names of the characters.

They then wrote comments which stated at least one good point and, if possible, one aspect to look out for in future work. Once this becomes a regular part of practice, it can be further developed to work on wider aspects of quality such as 'exciting first sentence' while the more simple criteria above became something they would self-evaluate against at regular times during each lesson. In one Year 1 class, each child had a 'handy hints' which was a laminated child's hand with a protruding finger. This finger was used to measure the correct sized gap between words. On the hand were written reminders like 'capital letter' 'full stop' 'finger space'. Each hand had up to three specific targets appropriate to the individual child which allowed for differentiation of these basic skills.

Visual success criteria are useful and teachers are increasingly using digital cameras to record work in progress which the children can refer to and compare their efforts against while still in the development stage. This has been particularly useful in practical subjects such as PE, where comparisons can be made in constructing a good headstand or forward roll. It is used equally effectively in design and technology, where products can be seen during the making process rather than by comparing completed objects at the end. In the Early Years setting, photographs help identify stages leading to 'good sitting' or 'good cloakrooms'. These are particularly useful when the children themselves have identified the stages involved in achieving quality and have used the technology themselves to capture the images. Equally effective are short video clips such as catching and throwing a ball or creating a series of on-balance and off-balance gymnastic sequences.

Other teachers have adapted the use of traffic light icons to help develop self-assessment skills. Children have labelled their work green, red or amber according to whether they thought they had good, partial or little understanding or displayed different coloured fans on their desk or cubes on top of their computers during the lessons to indicate their confidence as learning was taking place. In one classroom, the teacher provided red, yellow and green boxes for the children to put their work in at the end of the session. This allowed her to approach her feedback and planning in a more organised way and so the self-assessment from the children was informing the next steps. Such a system also provides information for the teacher about individual pupil's confidence levels with particular ideas and topics. Clearly, if many select red, then the teacher soon realises that this is work that needs to be revisited and reworked to gain better understanding. Conversely, a plethora of greens indicates that understanding is good and the class is ready to move onto more challenging work. A mixture of red, green and amber calls for different action

and often teachers would pair up green and amber students to talk about work, leaving the teacher free to deal with the more serious problems that the red pupils were having. The teacher can therefore map the pace and content of future work according to the children's needs at the time. It helps them actively grasp the responsibility for learning and so reduces their dependency on the teacher.

Giving responsibility to document learning to the learners clearly signals to the children that they have a definite role to play in deciding the learning journey. In one SEN/MLD school, each child was helped to use a video camera to record their work over the course of the week. Teachers helped them throughout the week to regularly reflect on practice in response to their personal targets in order to help the children develop self-regulatory skills. On the Friday of each week, the group watched a three-minute clip from the video evidence and heard a commentary from each learner. They then agreed whether targets had been met, or partly met, and redefined the targets for the next week.

8. Formative use of summative assessment

While the last decade has drawn teachers' attention to what is needed for good formative practice, there remains a need to continually reflect on how assessment practices affect the learning process, both directly by what teachers choose to do and indirectly through the messages these approaches leave with children about what we value in learning.

There remains confusion about the differences between formative and summative assessment with a view that summative is about testing. Put simply, summative assessment is a summary of attainment at a given point in time, often using standardised statements of attainment and recorded as a level or grade. Tests are often used to get this information. Formative assessment on the other hand is an ongoing planned process that focuses on identifying the next steps for improvement. Both types of assessment are needed, with the emphasis being on formative as the regular day-to-day practice. Summative assessment is required when decisions need to be made or for reporting to parents. Schools need to consider the best source for this summative information as tests provide only a small sample of a child's achievement over the course of a year.

Research by Harlen & Deakin-Crick, 2004, highlights a number of reasons as to why schools should think carefully about the amount and type of summative assessment they do. They argue that testing inhibits the quality of curriculum and the range of teaching strategies that teachers use in their classrooms. They also conclude that testing is found to be a demotivating factor, particularly for lower attainers, and shifts the emphasis from learning to performativity. On more pragmatic grounds, overuse of tests takes up a lot of valuable learning time both in giving the test and in preparation for it. For many schools, a formative approach requires a reduction in testing.

Formative assessment:	Summative assessment:
Mainly about improvement	Mainly about accountability
Looks forward	Looks backwards
Favours descriptive feedback	Favours tests and scores
Informs on quality	Samples knowledge
Can lead to improvements in learning	If overused, can have a negative impact

Teachers and parents are all too aware of the demoralising effect of over-testing on children and the inevitable narrowing of the curriculum as time is spent on preparing and doing testing. Children rapidly learn to identify themselves as 'winners or losers', especially when the children are referred to in terms of levels: 'You are level 3b in writing . . .' rather than recognised for their rate of progress over time: 'Your sentences are now more varied and most show a clear purpose. . .'. This focus on performativity becomes even more problematic if children are openly ranked and grouped in response to test outcomes.

Advice from the Assessment Reform Group states that:

. . . summative assessment should interfere as little as possible with teaching methods and the curriculum and, importantly, should reflect the full range of learning outcomes, particularly those needed for continued learning and for learning how to learn. Assessment by teachers has the potential for providing summative information about students' achievement since teachers can build up a picture of students' attainments across the full range of activities and goals. (Harlen, 2004)

Considerable money and expertise has been used to develop the many summative tests that children take in schools. The teachers in the original King's secondary project used items from external tests as tools to be used formatively in the classroom. This is an idea that primary teachers have further developed. Instead of asking children to attempt practice tests, specific questions, identified as causing most problems for the class were selected. Children worked on these difficult questions in pairs so that they were able to overcome the

problems collaboratively. For some questions, the teacher dealt with serious gaps in understanding by revisiting the concepts and ideas behind the questions. This allowed for a good balance between peer support and teacher mediation and generally encouraged a more active formative approach to test questions.

Some teachers start topics with a mind mapping session that helps the children to share what they know, partly know and do not yet know. From this, the teacher can plan sessions that are appropriate to their next steps in learning. Again, pace and content of the teaching can be matched to children's needs and so better learning is likely to take place. At the end of the topic, the children return to the mind map and add to it the learning that has taken place over the course of the topic. This celebrates learning and gives individual children a sense of progress and another opportunity to reflect on their own learning journey. The end-of-topic mind map can also be used for summative purposes since it notes the achievement made and also provides information about the class learning for the next teacher.

9. Learning together: learning from others

The approach we have taken in working with teachers and schools over the last decade stems from advice given in the review *Inside the Black Box* (Black & Wiliam, 1998b):

Teachers will not take up attractive sounding ideas, albeit based on extensive research, if these are presented as general principles which leave entirely to them the task of translating them into everyday practice – their classroom lives are too busy and fragile for this to be possible for all but the outstanding few. What they need is a variety of examples of implementation, by teachers with whom they can identify and from whom they can both derive conviction and confidence that they can do better, and see concrete examples of what doing better means in practice. . . . The essential first step is to set up a small number of local groups of schools . . . with each committed to a school based development and to collaboration within their local group. . . . The schools involved would need extra support, both to give their teachers time to plan the initiative in light of existing evidence, to reflect on their experience as it develops, and to advise on training work for others in the future.

(Black & Wiliam 1998, p. 15–16)

Professional development courses and projects have evolved at national and local level to help teachers improve their assessment practices. While research has been done by the King's College team on the effects of developing formative practice in classrooms (Black et al. 2002, 2003), their approach has looked mainly at schools which they have worked with directly, and only a few studies have inquired more broadly into the effects of professional development on formative practice in schools. In 2007, the 8 Schools Project reported on focused internal reviews of current Assessment for Learning practice carried out through an action research project by eight secondary schools completed by senior leaders in each of the schools. They found that practice varied widely across each school, and within departments, and the schools were then supported by consultants from the National Strategy team to set up an 18-month developmental project to help their teachers move their practice forward. Details of this can be found on the web (DCSF, 2008a). Development in primary schools tends to be easier to establish than in secondary schools because of the number of teachers to bring on board. Also, primary teachers work with the same children most of the time so they can be more flexible in helping the children to make changes in their learning behaviours. Most teachers begin by developing the assessment for learning ideas in one curricular area and then, as they gain confidence, bring in other curricular areas.

Assessment for learning requires changes in the ways teachers work with learners, which some may find risky, and which will certainly be challenging at times. The process is like a voyage of discovery, a journey into new territories of teaching and learning. For such a voyage, one needs the support of companions. Research evidence on teacher change concur that deep-rooted changes are difficult and generally take considerable time and effort to achieve (Fullan, 2003). Seng & Scharmer (2001) argue that creating such a system requires action on three levels:

1. Establishing a shared statement of purpose and a shared set of guiding principles.
2. Developing infrastructures that support community building.
3. Undertaking collaborative projects that focus on key change issues that create concrete projects for further deepening common purpose and improving infrastructures. (p. 242)

So, moving teachers forward in a sustainable fashion requires more than supporting individual teachers, but rather, requires programmes that encourage **professional communities of practice** that involve both teachers and senior leaders in schools. Developing a shared understanding of how assessment for learning works in the classroom and how formative practice functions alongside other demands on teachers' time is essential for any change to be achieved

in the long term. The vital element here is that the team must be helped to find time, to regularly talk with one another, at length, to share experiences, successes and disappointments, and also to observe one another's classroom work. They should also have access to outside advice, whether from their local authority or from others with experience in formative work. The plan for development should extend beyond the first year of implementation and provide opportunities for reflection and refocusing.

To help this process, we usually ask teachers to keep a Learning Diary and ask them to make entries during professional days, when planning formative lessons and after assessment for learning experiences with their classes. Teachers share ideas from their Learning Diaries when they meet, and towards the end of the school year, we ask them to describe their Learning Journey, noting the high and low points, the vital sessions or specific lessons which helped them change their practice. This self-reflection is both motivational and useful since it helps them decide how to move their practice forward for the following year, when they will have a new class but be starting from a different level of expertise in their formative practice.

The aim of any developmental programme should be to achieve

sustainable systems within each classroom which implement a proactive drive to take practice forward. It is important that any new practice developed is resilient enough to withstand future changes in curriculum, testing and staffing. The main aim is to build on the practice that is already established in teachers' classrooms and to help them **focus on the impact that formative practice has on learning** and specifically, on learning behaviours. At first, it seems a simple task to decide on next steps in learning, but when teachers start to explore children's understanding more carefully, they become more aware of the misunderstandings that they need to unravel, the differentiated approach they need to take with different groups of learners and how the pace of future learning is dependent on confidence in the current learning. The main hope is that, through supporting teachers in becoming both proactive and reflective in exploring children's understanding by either trying new strategies or strengthening established ones, they will become more aware of how to respond to their learners' needs. This will help them feel more confident that they can take the formative action required to move learning forward and to facilitate improvement and progress. A key feature of such a project will be encouraging the interactions and relationship between senior managers and classroom teachers as teachers start to work on moving their formative practice forward so that there is a **shared understanding of the steps needed to make the initiative successful**.

The creation of an environment in which formative practice flourishes requires teachers to weigh up and assess how effective talk is employed in their classroom, how confident and enthusiastic their pupils are to 'have a go' at learning and how well peers support and challenge one another when engaged in collaborative learning. So it is not simply a matter of teachers adopting assessment for learning strategies, but rather thinking through how they can create learning scenarios that offer opportunities to cue pupils into learning expectations and provide feedback as the learning is taking place. It is how teachers provide guidance to help pupils learn and how teachers structure and facilitate those activities that enable learning. What matters here is that the approach is tailored to particular groups of learners and so it is the teacher who decides how to manage and facilitate the formative classroom. In other words, it is **consistency of principle not uniformity of practice** that works. While teachers might prefer to work together on developing a particular strategy, it is how they personally adapt this to work for their children that counts.

The changes in practice recommended here are not easily made by everyone. Teachers need to familiarise themselves with new ideas and to understand their implications for themselves as teachers and for their learners in the classroom before they adopt and adapt them. Our take on professional learning runs in a similar vein to that of our assessment for learning principles. We recognise that many primary teachers are creative and inventive and very skilled in group management. However, developing new practices is a risky business and one that will call on teacher time and effort to ensure that they are not only effective but seen as acceptable within the school context (Loucks-Horsley et al, 2003). Such developments frequently take place in environments where there are competing priorities for teacher time and development of practice (Harrison, 2005) and so it is essential that teachers attempting to change their practice do so in an environment of strong peer and senior leadership support and encouragement. In most cases, it is important to recognise what changes need to be made and then to hone and refine practice and to have the courage to abandon some practices that have been superseded by the children's newly developed independent learning skills.

Evaluation is a vital part of any plan. This should be on-going, in terms of mutual observation and of sharing of ideas and resources to support professional learning. It might also be summative; evidence of experience and test results of pupils might be collected at certain stages and perhaps supplemented with evaluation by colleagues not directly involved.

References

Alexander, R. (2004) *Towards Dialogic Teaching: rethinking classroom talk.* Cambridge: Dialogos.

Assessment Reform Group (1999) *Assessment for learning: Beyond the black box.* Available at www.assessment-reform-group.org/

Black, P. & Wiliam, D. (1998a) Assessment and Classroom Learning *Assessment in Education: Principles Policy and Practice,* **5** (1), pp.7–73.

Black, P. & Wiliam, D (1998b) *Inside the black box: Raising standards through classroom assessment.* London: GL Assessment.

Black, P., Harrison, C., Lee, C., Marshall, B. & Wiliam, D. (2002) *Working inside the black box: assessment for learning in the classroom.* London: GL Assessment.

Black, P., Harrison, C., Lee, C., Marshall, B. & Wiliam, D. (2003) *Assessment for Learning: putting it into practice.* London: Open University Press.

Butler, R. (1987) Task-Involving and Ego-Involving Properties of

Evaluation: Effects of Different Feedback Conditions on Motivational Perceptions, Interest and Performance. *Journal of Educational Psychology*, **79** (4), pp. 474–482.

Clarke, S. (2001) *Unlocking Formative Assessment*. London: Hodder.

DCELLS (2008) *Framework for Children's Learning for 3 to 7-year-olds in Wales*. Cardiff: Department for Children, Education and Life Long Learning Skills.

DCSF (2008a) Assessment for Learning (AfL) 8 Schools Project Report. London: Department for Children, Schools and Families. Available at www.standards. dcsf.gov.uk/secondary/keystage3/afl8.

DCSF (2008b) *Statutory Framework for Early Years Foundation Stage*. London: Department for Children, Schools and Families.

DCSF (2008c) *The Primary Framework*. Available at www.standards.dfes.gov.uk/ primaryframeworks/

DfES (2003) *Excellence and Enjoyment: A strategy for primary schools*; London: Department for Education and Skills.

Dweck, C. (2000). *Self theories: Their role in motivation, personality, and development*. London: Taylor and Francis.

EPPE (2004) *Effective Provision of Pre-School Education: Final Report*. Available at www. surestart.gov.uk/research/ keyresearch/ eppe/.

Fullan, M. (2003) *The Moral Imperative of School Leadership*. Thousand Oaks, CA: Corwin Press.

Harlen, W. (2004) A systematic review of the evidence of reliability and validity of assessment by teachers used for summative purposes. *Research Evidence in Education Library*. London: EPPI-Centre, Social Science Research Unit, Institute of Education, University of London.

Harlen, W. & Deakin-Crick, R. (2004) *Testing, Learning & Motivation*. Cambridge: Assessment Reform Group.

Harrison, C (2005) Teachers Development of Assessment for Learning: mapping teacher change. *Journal of Teacher Development*, 9 (2). pp 255–263.

Loucks-Horsley, S., Love, N., Stiles, K, Mundry, S. & Hewson, P. (2003) *Designing Professional Development for Teachers of Science and Mathematics 2nd Edition*. Thousand Oaks, CA: Corwin Press.

Rowe, M. (1974) Wait time and rewards as instructional variables, their influence on language, logic and fate control. *Journal of Research in Science Teaching*, **11**, pp. 81–94

Senge, P. & Sharmer, O. (2001) Community Action Research; Learning as a Community of Practitioners, Consultants and Researchers. In: Reason P, Bradbury H (eds), *Handbook of action research: Participative inquiry and practice*. London: Sage Publications.

University of Cambridge (2008) *The Primary Review: The condition and future of primary education in England.* Available at www.primaryreview.org.uk/index.html

Vygotsky, L (1978) *Mind in Society*, Cambridge: Massachusetts: Harvard University Press.